SPECTRUM®

Uppercase Letters

PreK–K

Published by Spectrum®
an imprint of Carson-Dellosa Publishing
Greensboro, NC

Spectrum®
An imprint of Carson-Dellosa Publishing LLC
P.O. Box 35665
Greensboro, NC 27425 USA

ISBN 978-1-4838-3099-5

01-053167784

Table of Contents

Recognizing Uppercase Letters

Writing Uppercase Letters

Find A

ANT

Directions: Help the ant find the picnic. Color the boxes with **A**.

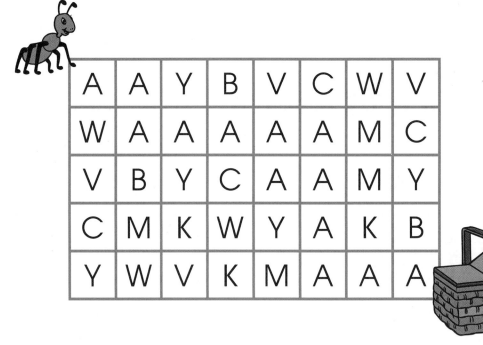

A	A	Y	B	V	C	W	V
W	A	A	A	A	A	M	C
V	B	Y	C	A	A	M	Y
C	M	K	W	Y	A	K	B
Y	W	V	K	M	A	A	A

Directions: Circle **A** in each word.

APPLE   HAT

Find B

 **B**

BED

Directions: Color the shapes with **B**.

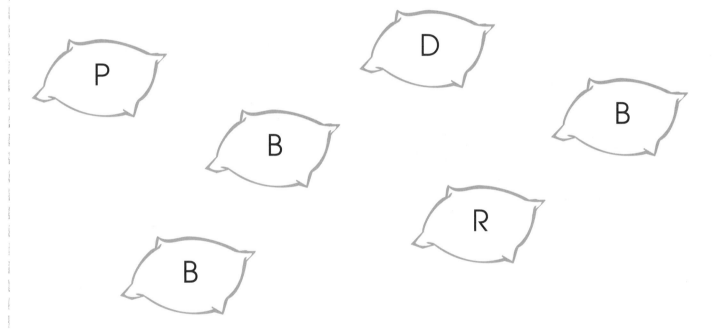

P

D

B

B

R

B

Directions: Circle **B** in each word.

BOOK

BEAR

Find C

  **COW**

Directions: Draw a line from the corn to the circles with **C**.

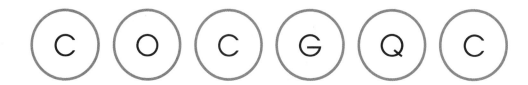

Directions: Circle **C** in each word.

CAT   SOCK

A B C **D** E F G H I J K L M N O P Q R S T U V W X Y Z

Find D

D **DOG**

Directions: Help the dog find the bone. Color the boxes with **D**.

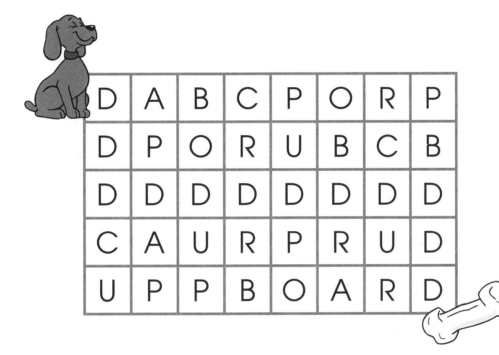

D	A	B	C	P	O	R	P
D	P	O	R	U	B	C	B
D	D	D	D	D	D	D	D
C	A	U	R	P	R	U	D
U	P	P	B	O	A	R	D

Directions: Circle **D** in each word.

DEER   RED

A B C D **E** F G H I J K L M N O P Q R S T U V W X Y Z

Find E

  **EGG**

Directions: Color the shapes with **E**.

Directions: Circle **E** in each word.

 TEN

 BELL

A B C D E  G H I J K L M N O P Q R S T U V W X Y Z

Find F

 **FAN**

Directions: Draw a line from the feather to the circles with **F**.

Directions: Circle **F** in each word.

FIVE

LEAF

A B C D E F  G H I J K L M N O P Q R S T U V W X Y Z

Find G

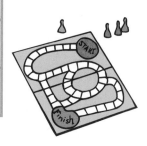  **GIRL**

Directions: Help the girl win the game. Color the boxes with **G**.

G	O	D	Q	D	C	D	O
G	C	C	Q	O	F	Q	A
G	A	Q	O	D	O	C	Q
G	C	O	Q	Q	C	D	O
G	G	G	G	G	G	G	G

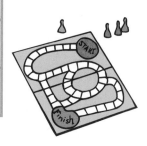

Directions: Circle **G** in each word.

GUITAR

RUG

A B C D E F G **H** I J K L M N O P Q R S T U V W X Y Z

Find H

  **HORSE**

Directions: Color the shapes with **H**.

E

H

I

H

E

F

Directions: Circle **H** in each word.

HOUSE

HORN

A B C D E F G H  J K L M N O P Q R S T U V W X Y Z

Find I

IGLOO

Directions: Draw a line from the igloo to the circles with **I**.

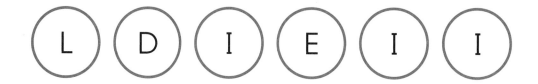

(L) (D) (I) (E) (I) (I)

Directions: Circle **I** in each word.

INK

6

SIX

A B C D E F G H I **J** K L M N O P Q R S T U V W X Y Z

Find J

  **JET**

Directions: Help the Jet fly. Start at the bottom. Color the boxes with **J**.

J	E	I	H	L	H	D	I
J	J	J	D	F	I	L	F
I	H	J	J	J	G	I	L
G	L	I	I	J	J	J	I
L	F	I	U	E	G	J	J

Directions: Circle **J** in each word.

 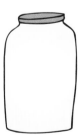

JACKET

JAR

A B C D E F G H I J  L M N O P Q R S T U V W X Y Z

Find K

 **KITE**

Directions: Color the shapes with **K**.

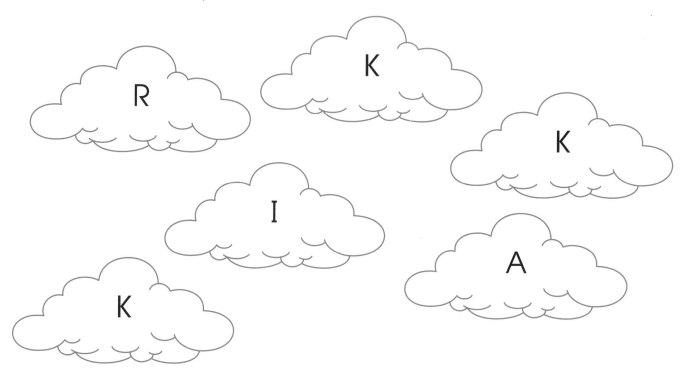

R

K

K

I

A

K

Directions: Circle **K** in each word.

KEY

LOCK

A B C D E F G H I J K **L** M N O P Q R S T U V W X Y Z

Find L

  **LION**

Directions: Draw a line from the ladder to the circles with **L**.

(E) (L) (T) (I) (L) (L)

Directions: Circle **L** in each word.

LETTERS

MAILBOX

A B C D E F G H I J K L **M** N O P Q R S T U V W X Y Z

Find M

  **MOON**

Directions: Help the rocket go to the moon. Start at the bottom. Color the boxes with **M**.

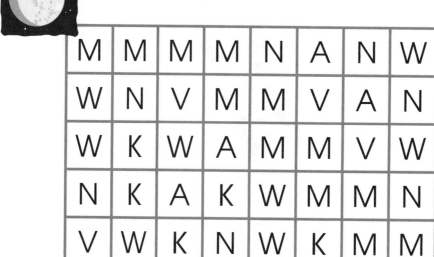

M	M	M	M	N	A	N	W
W	N	V	M	M	V	A	N
W	K	W	A	M	M	V	W
N	K	A	K	W	M	M	N
V	W	K	N	W	K	M	M

Directions: Circle **M** in each word.

MOUSE

DRUM

A B C D E F G H I J K L M  N O P Q R S T U V W X Y Z

Find N

 **N**EST

N

Directions: Color the shapes with **N**.

 M

 N

 M

 N

 V

 H

Directions: Circle **N** in each word.

NUT

9

NINE

A B C D E F G H I J K L M N **O** P Q R S T U V W X Y Z

Find O

  **OCTOPUS**

Directions: Draw a line from the octopus to the circles with **O**.

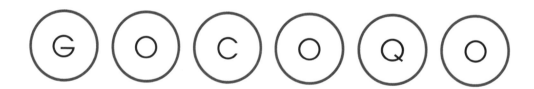

G O C O Q O

Directions: Circle **O** in each word.

OLIVES

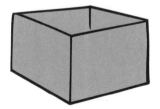

BOX

Find P

 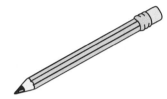 **PENCIL**

Directions: Help the pencil write on the paper. Color the boxes with **P**.

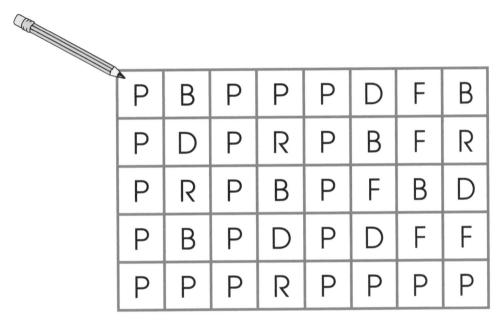

P	B	P	P	P	D	F	B
P	D	P	R	P	B	F	R
P	R	P	B	P	F	B	D
P	B	P	D	P	D	F	F
P	P	P	R	P	P	P	P

Directions: Circle **P** in each word.

PIG   MOP

Find Q

  **Q**UILT

Directions: Color the shapes with **Q**.

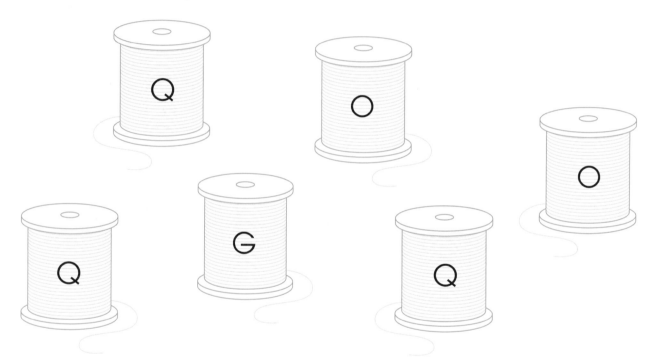

Directions: Circle **Q** in each word.

QUARTER

QUACK

Find R

  **RAINBOW**

Directions: Draw a line from the raindrops to the circles with **R**.

R   B   R   P   D   R

Directions: Circle **R** in each word.

RING   CAR

Find S

  **SUN**

Directions: Help the sun shine on the flower. Color the boxes with **S**.

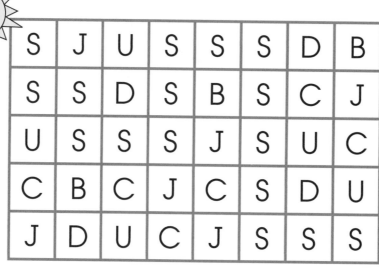

S	J	U	S	S	S	D	B
S	S	D	S	B	S	C	J
U	S	S	S	J	S	U	C
C	B	C	J	C	S	D	U
J	D	U	C	J	S	S	S

Directions: Circle **S** in each word.

HOSE

BUS

A B C D E F G H I J K L M N O P Q R S **T** U V W X Y Z

Find T

 **T**  **TENT**

Directions: Color the shapes with **T**.

Directions: Circle **T** in each word.

TURTLE   NUT

Find U

  **UMBRELLA**

Directions: Draw a line from the umbrella to the circles with **U**.

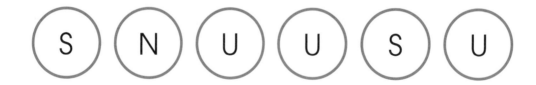

S N U U S U

Directions: Circle **U** in each word.

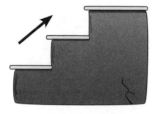

UP

MUG

Find V

  **VAN**

Directions: Help the van get home. Color the boxes with **V**.

V	W	N	M	V	V	V	V
V	N	W	X	V	W	N	V
V	W	X	N	V	N	N	V
V	V	V	V	V	W	X	V
M	W	N	X	W	M	N	V

Directions: Circle **V** in each word.

VASE   VEST

Find W

  **WEB**

Directions: Color the shapes with **W**.

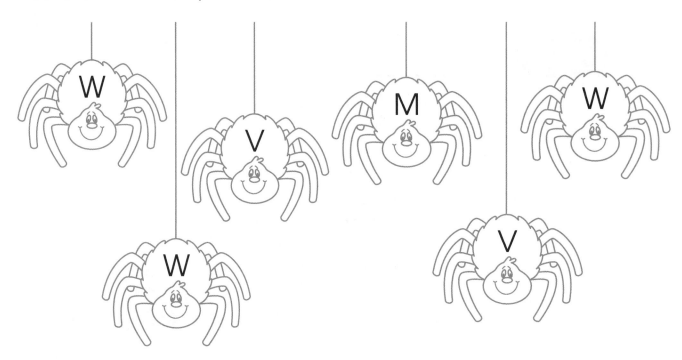

Directions: Circle **W** in each word.

WORM

WELL

A B C D E F G H I J K L M N O P Q R S T U V W **X** Y Z

Find X

  **FOX**

Directions: Draw a line from the fox to the circles with **X**.

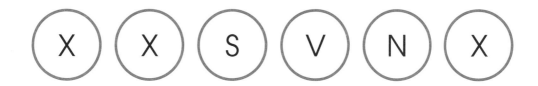

(X) (X) (S) (V) (N) (X)

Directions: Circle **X** in each word.

SIX

AX

Find Y

  **YARN**

Directions: Color the shapes with **Y**.

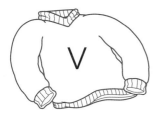
V

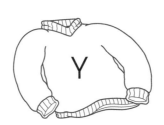
Y

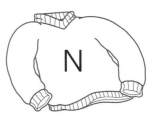
N

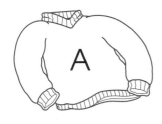
A

V

Y

Directions: Circle **Y** in each word.

YARD

YO-YO

A B C D E F G H I J K L M N O P Q R S T U V W X Y **Z**

Find Z

  **ZEBRA**

Directions: Help the zebra get to the zoo. Color the boxes with **Z**.

Z	Z	Z	Z	Z	Z	Z	X
X	A	V	N	X	N	Z	V
Z	Z	Z	Z	Z	Z	Z	V
Z	X	V	X	A	N	A	X
Z	Z	Z	Z	Z	Z	Z	Z

Directions: Circle **Z** in each word.

ZIPPER

PUZZLE

A B C D E F G H I J K L M N O P Q R S T U V W X Y Z

Review

Directions: In each row, circle the letter that is the same as the first letter in the row.

G	O	R	G	B
M	T	P	Y	M
R	N	B	R	I
B	B	O	Y	P
W	A	M	W	B
J	U	C	J	B
T	T	I	L	E

A B C D E F G H I J K L M N O P Q R S T U V W X Y Z

Review

Directions: In each row, circle the letter that is the same as the first letter in the row.

A	Y	A	V	N
D	P	B	D	R
K	W	A	Z	K
F	E	T	H	F
Q	Q	O	G	C
C	O	G	C	Q
S	U	S	J	M

A B C D E F G H I J K L M N O P Q R S T U V W X Y Z

I Know My ABCs

Directions: Point to each letter as you sing the ABCs. Say the name of each picture. Color the pictures.

A  **B**  **C**

D  **E**

F  **G**  **H**

I  **J**

K  **L**  **M**

Uppercase Letters PreK–K

A B C D E F G H I J K L M N O P Q R S T U V W X Y Z

I Know My ABCs

Directions: Point to each letter as you sing the ABCs. Say the name of each picture. Color the pictures.

N  O  P

Q  R

S  T  U

V  W

X  Y  Z

Uppercase Letters PreK–K

I Know My ABCs

Directions: Help the dog find its house. Connect the letters in ABC order.

A B C D E F G H I J K L M N O P Q R S T U V W X Y Z

I Know My ABCs

Directions: Connect the dots in ABC order.

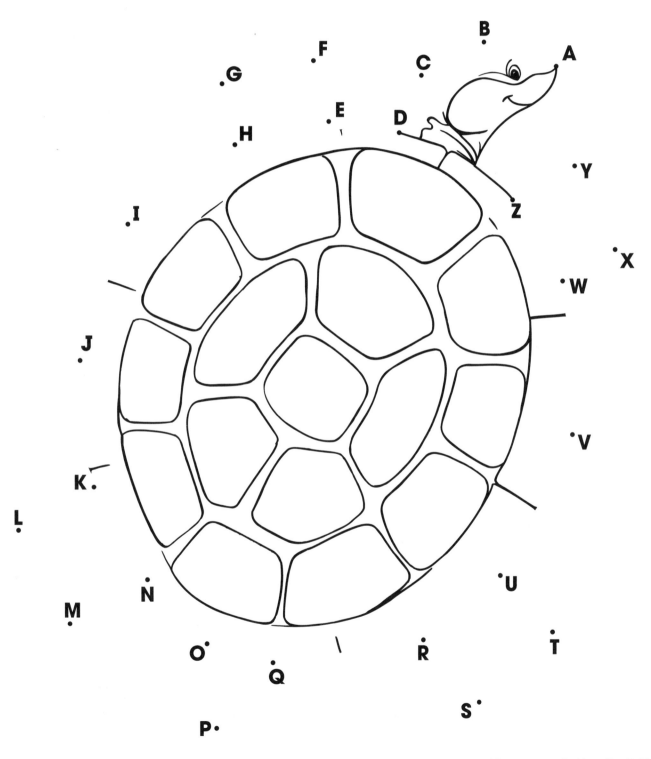

A B C D E F G H I J K L M N O P Q R S T U V W X Y Z

Write Lines From Top to Bottom

Directions: Trace each line from top to bottom. Begin at ●.

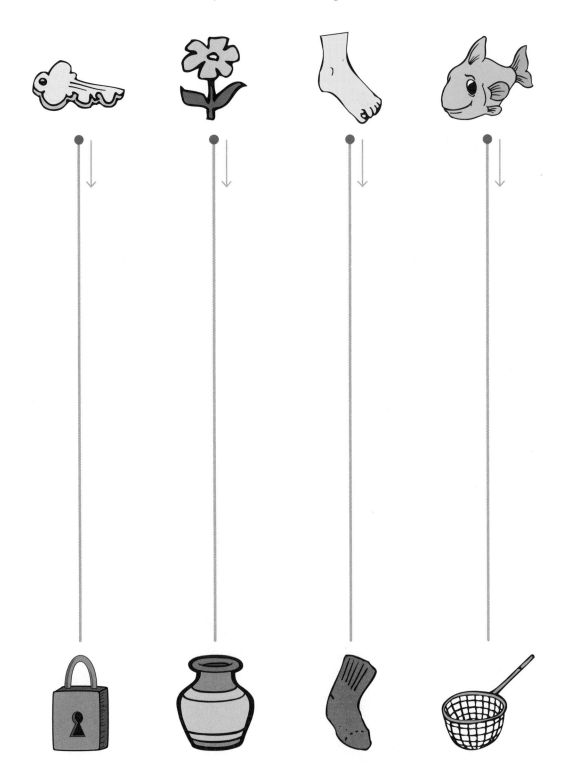

Write Lines From Left to Right

Directions: Trace each line from left to right. Begin at ●.

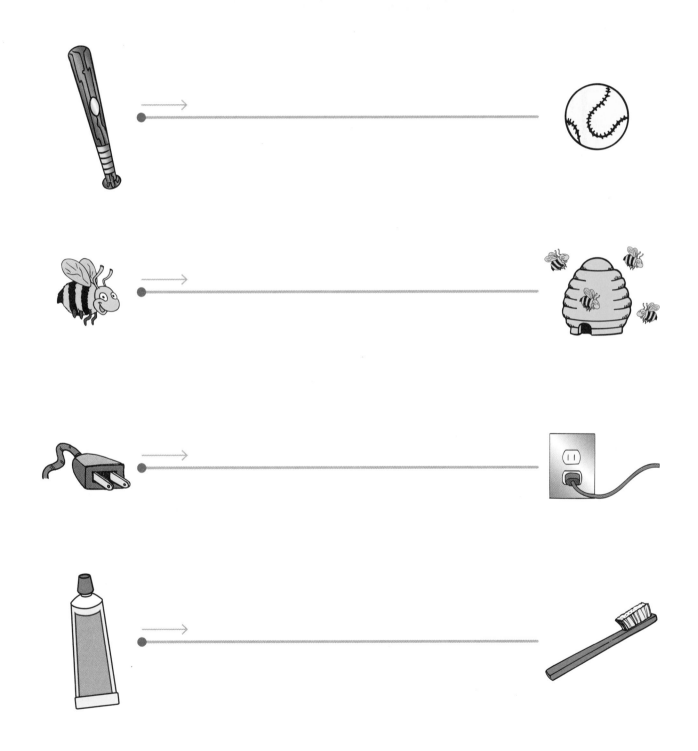

A B C D E F G H I J K L M N O P Q R S T U V W X Y Z

Write Lines From Top to Bottom and Left to Right

Directions: Trace each line from top to bottom or from left to right. Begin at ●.

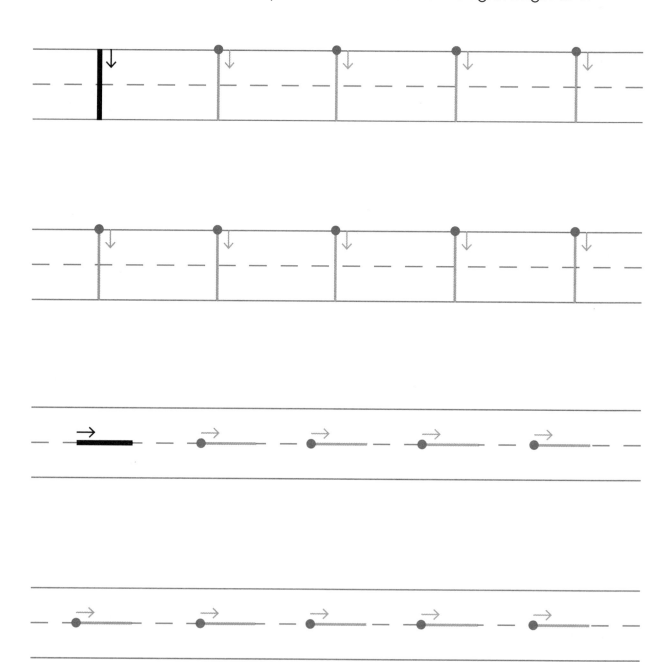

Write L

Directions: Look at the letter and the arrows. Then, trace and write the letter. Begin at ●.

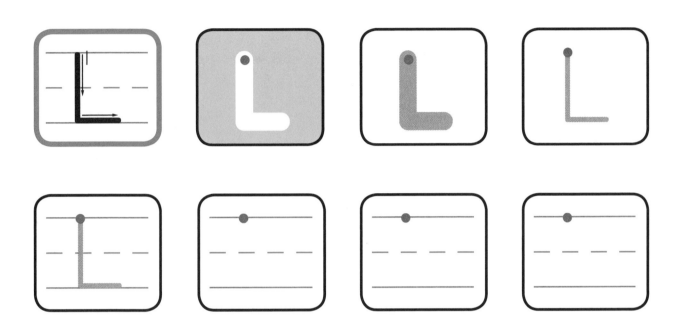

Directions: Write **L** to complete the words.

___ION

___IPS

A B C D E F G H I J K L M N O P Q R S **T** U V W X Y Z

Write T

Directions: Look at the letter and the arrows. Then, trace and write the letter. Begin at ●.

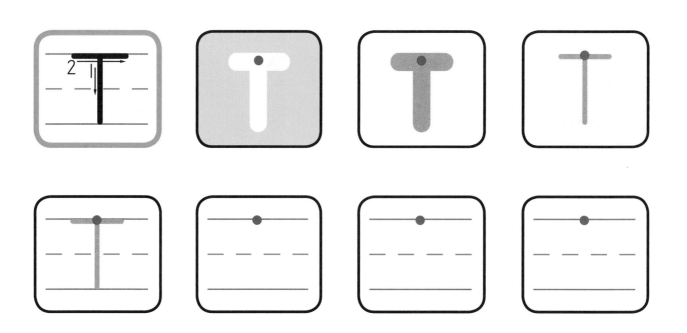

Directions: Write **T** to complete the words.

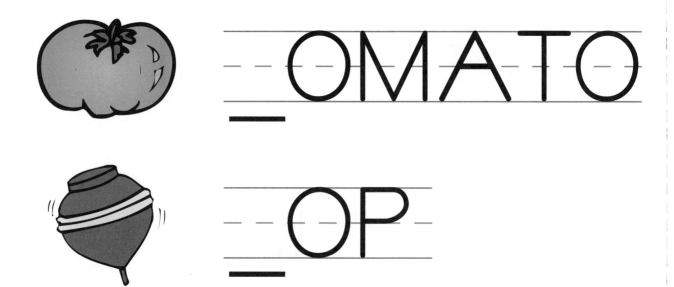

_OMATO

_OP

A B C D E F G H **I** J K L M N O P Q R S T U V W X Y Z

Write I

Directions: Look at the letter and the arrows. Then, trace and write the letter. Begin at ●.

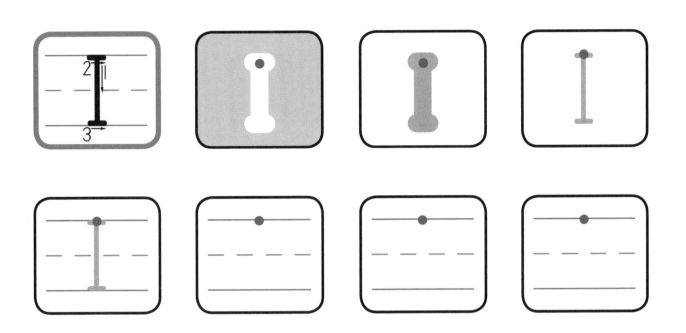

Directions: Write **I** to complete the words.

M_LK

F_SH

A B C D E F G **H** I J K L M N O P Q R S T U V W X Y Z

Write H

Directions: Look at the letter and the arrows. Then, trace and write the letter. Begin at ●.

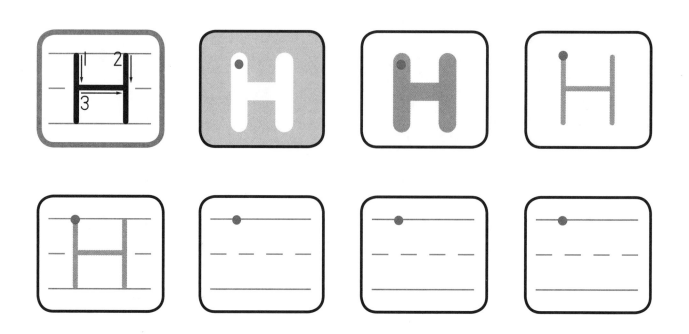

Directions: Write **H** to complete the words.

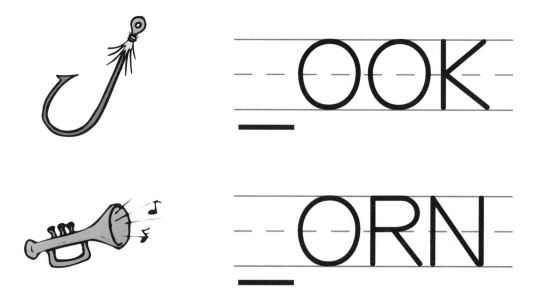

__OOK

__ORN

Write F

Directions: Look at the letter and the arrows. Then, trace and write the letter. Begin at ●.

Directions: Write **F** to complete the words.

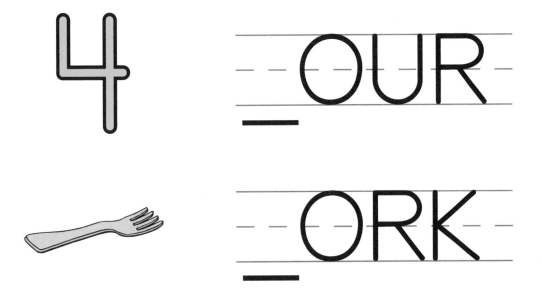

4 _OUR

_ORK

A B C D **E** F G H I J K L M N O P Q R S T U V W X Y Z

Write E

Directions: Look at the letter and the arrows. Then, trace and write the letter. Begin at ●.

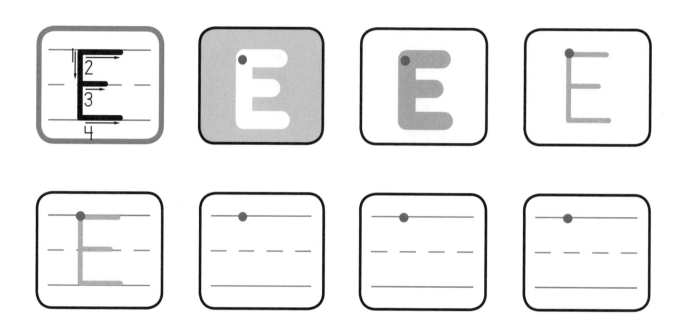

Directions: Write **E** to complete the words.

A B C D E F G H I J K L M N O P Q R S T U V W X Y Z

Review

Directions: Write a letter from the box to complete each word.

E   F   H   I   L   T

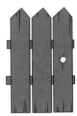

_ ENCE

B _ B

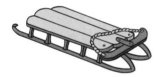

SL _ D

_ OG

_ IGER

_ OSE

Write Slanted Lines

Directions: Trace each line from top to bottom. Begin at ●.

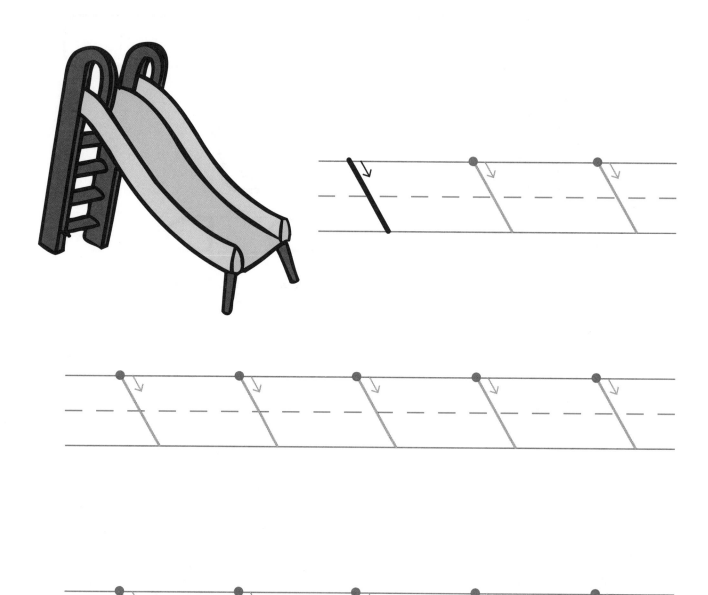

Write Slanted Lines

Directions: Trace each line. Begin at ●.

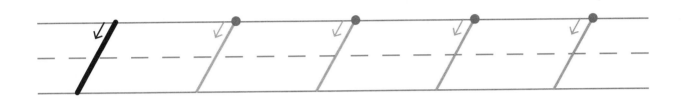

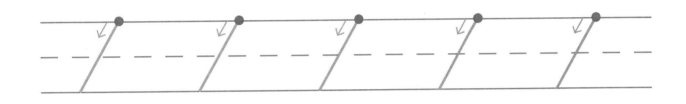

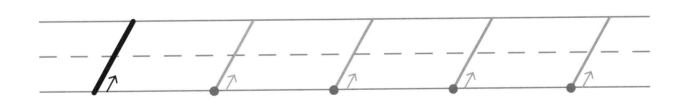

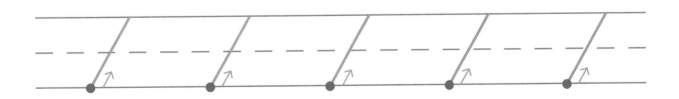

Write A

Directions: Look at the letter and the arrows. Then, trace and write the letter. Begin at ●.

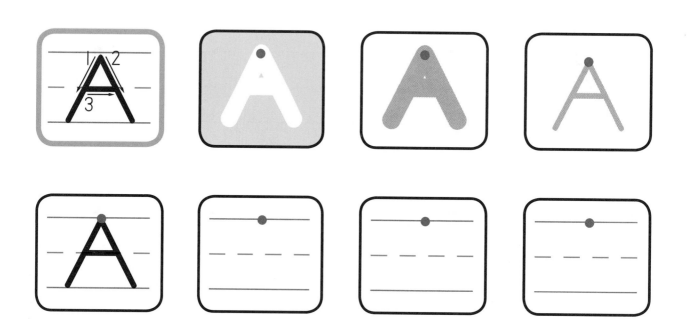

Directions: Write **A** to complete the words.

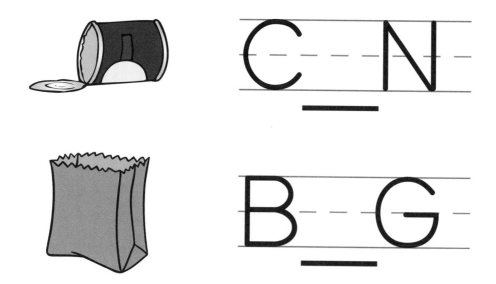

C _ N

B _ G

A B C D E F G H I J **K** L M N O P Q R S T U V W X Y Z

Write K

Directions: Look at the letter and the arrows. Then, trace and write the letter. Begin at ●.

Directions: Write **K** to complete the words.

DUC___

___ING

A B C D E F G H I J K L M N O P Q R S T U V W **X** Y Z

Write X

Directions: Look at the letter and the arrows. Then, trace and write the letter. Begin at ●.

Directions: Write **X** to complete the words.

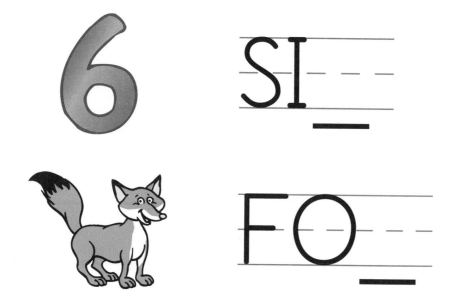

Write Y

Directions: Look at the letter and the arrows. Then, trace and write the letter. Begin at ●.

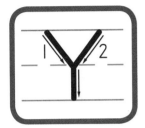   

Directions: Write **Y** to complete the words.

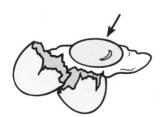

BO __

__OLK

A B C D E F G H I J K L M N O P Q R S T U V W X Y **Z**

Write Z

Directions: Look at the letter and the arrows. Then, trace and write the letter. Begin at ●.

Directions: Write **Z** to complete the words.

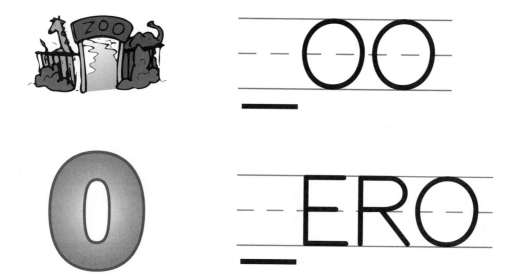

_OO

_ERO

A B C D E F G H I J K L M **N** O P Q R S T U V W X Y Z

Write N

Directions: Look at the letter and the arrows. Then, trace and write the letter. Begin at •.

Directions: Write **N** to complete the words.

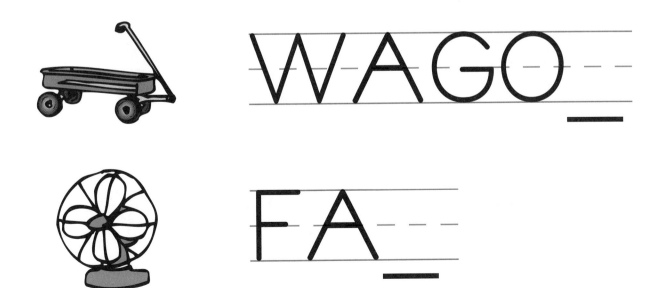

WAGO_

FA_

Write M

Directions: Look at the letter and the arrows. Then, trace and write the letter. Begin at ●.

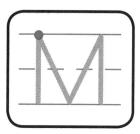 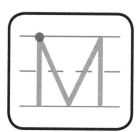 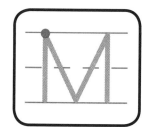 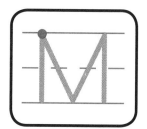

Directions: Write **M** to complete the words.

_ASK

HA_

A B C D E F G H I J K L M N O P Q R S T U **V** W X Y Z

Write V

Directions: Look at the letter and the arrows. Then, trace and write the letter. Begin at ●.

Directions: Write **V** to complete the words.

_INE

DI_E

A B C D E F G H I J K L M N O P Q R S T U V **W** X Y Z

Write W

Directions: Look at the letter and the arrows. Then, trace and write the letter. Begin at ●.

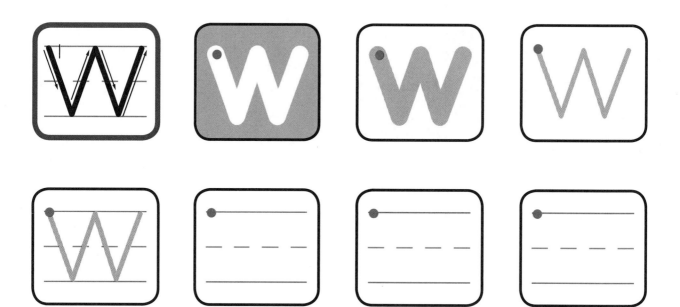

Directions: Write **W** to complete the words.

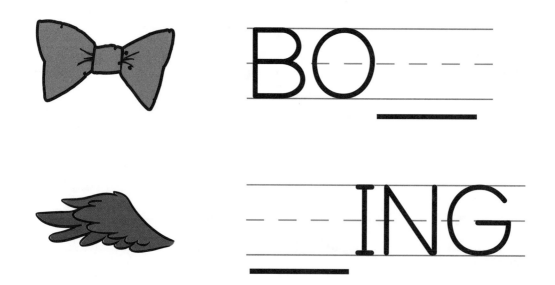

BO___

___ING

A B C D E F G H I J K L M N O P Q R S T U V W X Y Z

Review

Directions: Write letters from the box to complete the words.

A K M N V W X Y Z

A __

__ IPPER

__ __

__ OR __

SOC __

__ ARN

Write Circle Lines

Directions: Trace each circle and half circle. Begin at ●.

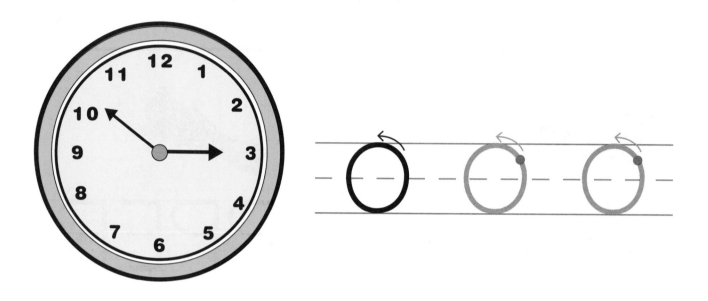

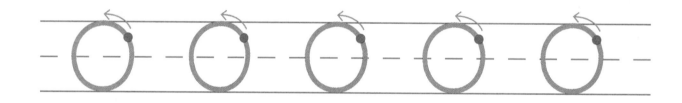

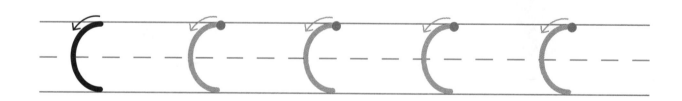

Name

A B C D E F G H I J K L M N **O** P Q R S T U V W X Y Z

Write O

Directions: Look at the letter and the arrows. Then, trace and write the letter. Begin at ●.

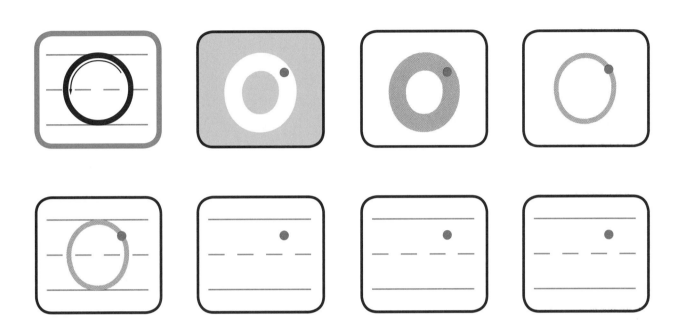

Directions: Write **O** to complete the words.

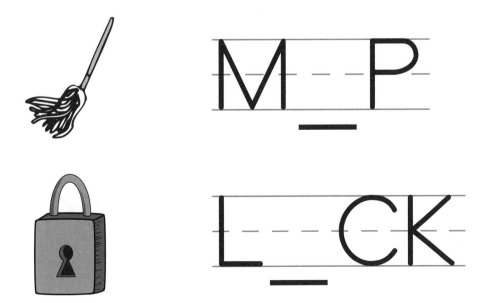

M_P

L_CK

A B C D E F G H I J K L M N O P **Q** R S T U V W X Y Z

Write Q

Directions: Look at the letter and the arrows. Then, trace and write the letter. Begin at ●.

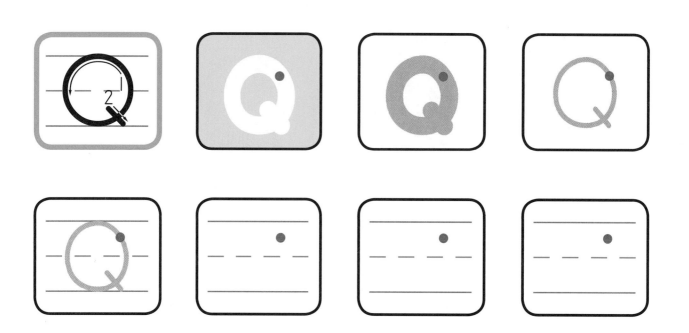

Directions: Write **Q** to complete the words.

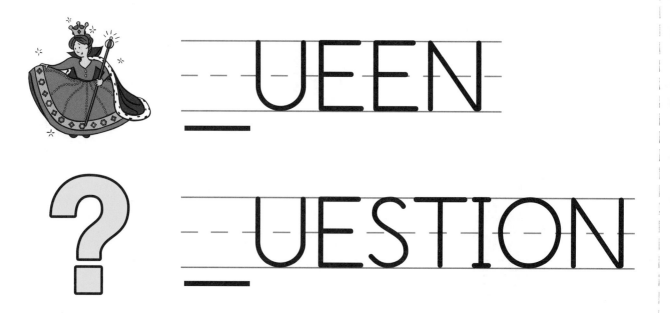

_UEEN

_UESTION

A B **C** D E F G H I J K L M N O P Q R S T U V W X Y Z

Write C

Directions: Look at the letter and the arrows. Then, trace and write the letter. Begin at ●.

Directions: Write **C** to complete the words.

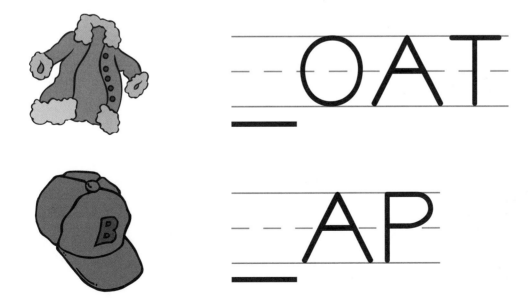

_OAT

_AP

A B C D E F **G** H I J K L M N O P Q R S T U V W X Y Z

Write G

Directions: Look at the letter and the arrows. Then, trace and write the letter. Begin at ●.

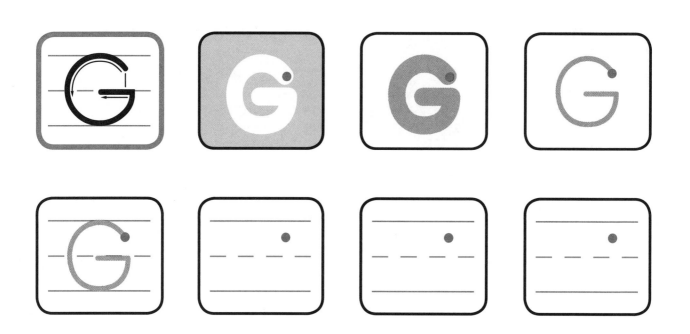

Directions: Write **G** to complete the words.

RU___

___AS

A B C D E F G H I J K L M N O P Q R S T U V W X Y Z

Review

Directions: Write letters from the box to complete the words.

| C | G | O | Q |

FRO __

__ OMB

P __ T

__ UILT

G __ AT

__ OOSE

Write Curved Lines

Directions: Trace the curved lines. Begin at ●.

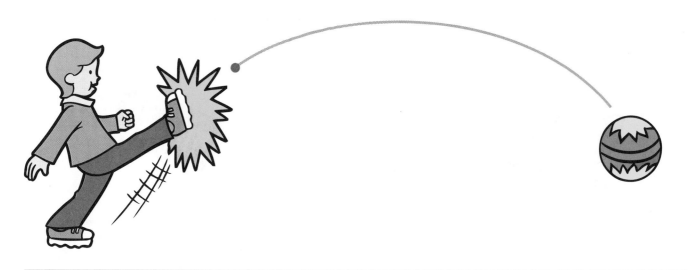

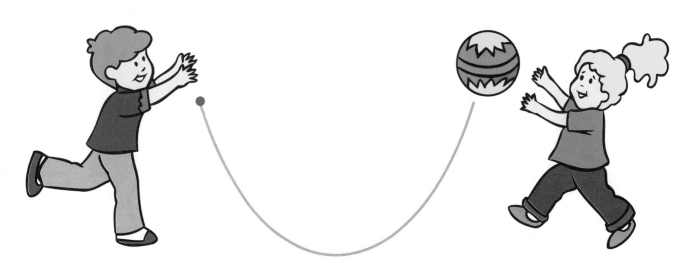

Write Curved Lines

Directions: Trace the curved lines. Begin at •.

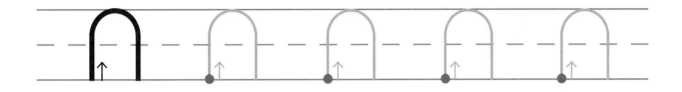

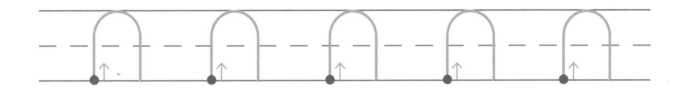

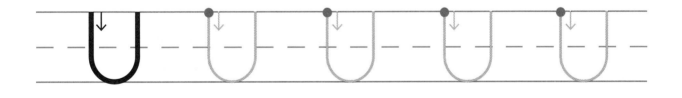

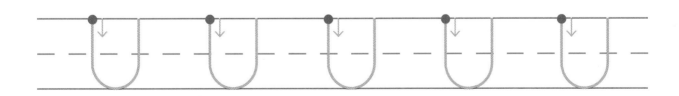

A B C **D** E F G H I J K L M N O P Q R S T U V W X Y Z

Write D

Directions: Look at the letter and the arrows. Then, trace and write the letter. Begin at ●.

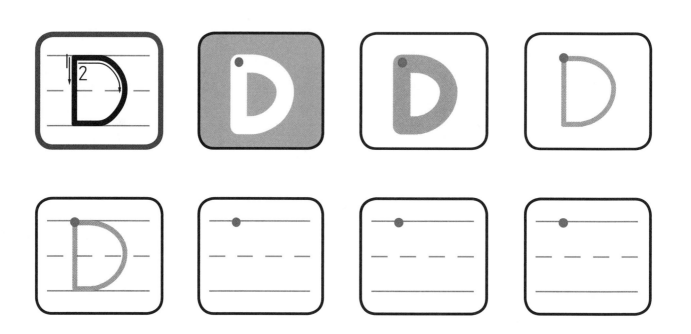

Directions: Write **D** to complete the words.

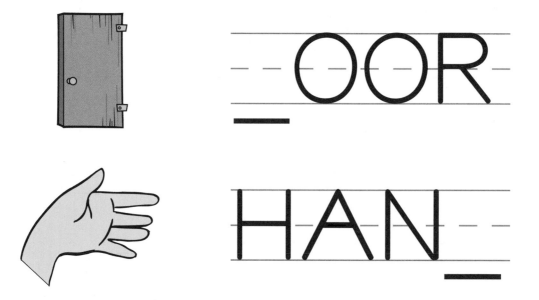

___OOR

HAN___

A B C D E F G H I J K L M N O **P** Q R S T U V W X Y Z

Write P

Directions: Look at the letter and the arrows. Then, trace and write the letter. Begin at ●.

Directions: Write **P** to complete the words.

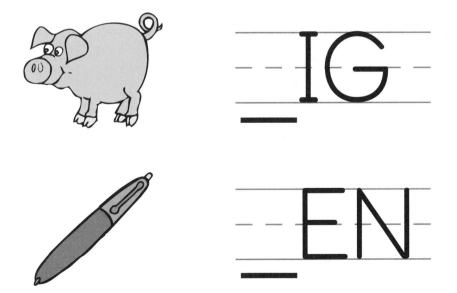

IG

EN

A B C D E F G H I J K L M N O P Q **R** S T U V W X Y Z

Write R

Directions: Look at the letter and the arrows. Then, trace and write the letter. Begin at ●.

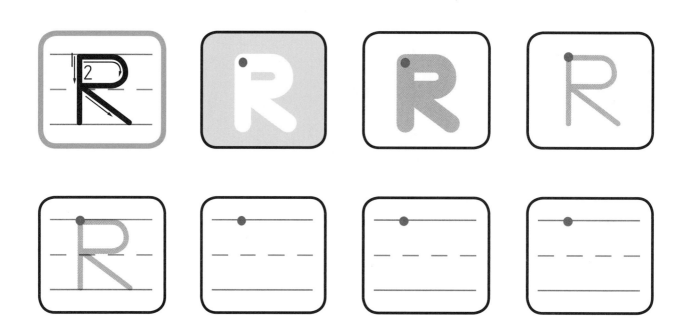

Directions: Write **R** to complete the words.

PEA__

__OSE

A **B** C D E F G H I J K L M N O P Q R S T U V W X Y Z

Write B

Directions: Look at the letter and the arrows. Then, trace and write the letter. Begin at ●.

Directions: Write **B** to complete the words.

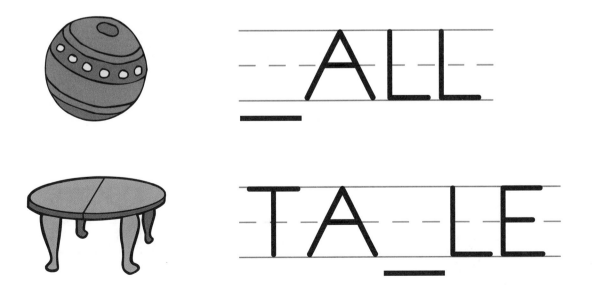

_ALL

TA_LE

A B C D E F G H I **J** K L M N O P Q R S T U V W X Y Z

Write J

Directions: Look at the letter and the arrows. Then, trace and write the letter. Begin at ●.

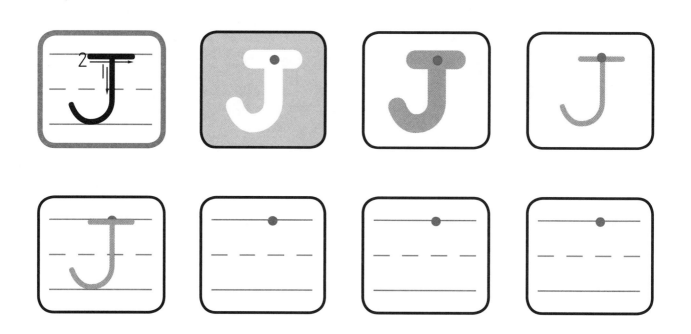

Directions: Write **J** to complete the words.

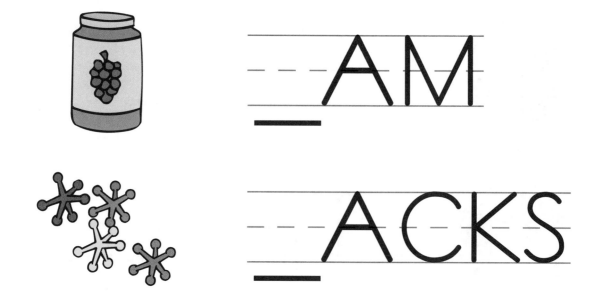

_ _ _ AM

_ _ _ ACKS

A B C D E F G H I J K L M N O P Q R S T **U** V W X Y Z

Write U

Directions: Look at the letter and the arrows. Then, trace and write the letter. Begin at ●.

Directions: Write **U** to complete the words.

BR_SH

 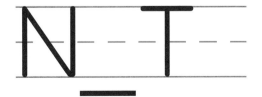

N_T

Write S

Directions: Look at the letter and the arrows. Then, trace and write the letter. Begin at ●.

Directions: Write **S** to complete the words.

_EAL

_EVEN

Review

Directions: Write letters from the box to complete the words.

B   D   J   P   R   S   U

EEP

___

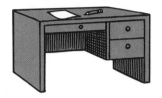

ESK

___

U

___

OOF

___

SOA

___

PL_G

___

A B C D E F G H I J K L M N O P Q R S T U V W X Y Z

Writing Review

Directions: Say the name of each picture. Write the uppercase letter that names its beginning sound.

Name_____

A B C D E F G H I J K L M N O P Q R S T U V W X Y Z

Writing Review

Directions: Say the name of each picture. Write the uppercase letter that names its beginning sound.

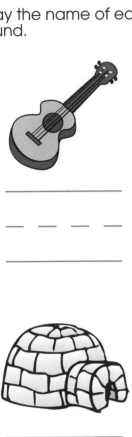

_____

_ _ _ _ _ _

_____

_____

_ _ _ _ _ _

_____

_____

_ _ _ _ _ _

_____

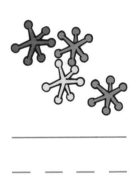

_____

_ _ _ _ _ _

_____

_____

_ _ _ _ _ _

_____

_____

_ _ _ _ _ _

_____

_____

_ _ _ _ _ _

_____

Writing Review

Directions: Say the name of each picture. Write the uppercase letter that names its beginning sound.

A B C D E F G H I J K L M N O P Q R S T U V W X Y Z

Writing Review

Directions: Say the name of each picture. Write the uppercase letter that names its beginning sound.

_____

- - - - - - - - -

_____

_____

- - - - - - - - -

_____

_____

- - - - - - - - -

_____

_____

- - - - - - - - -

_____

_____

- - - - - - - - -

_____

Answer Key

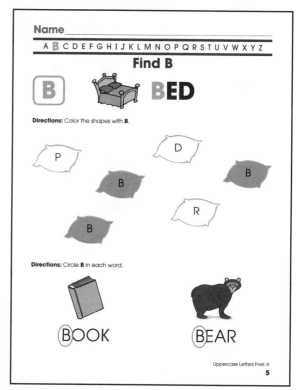

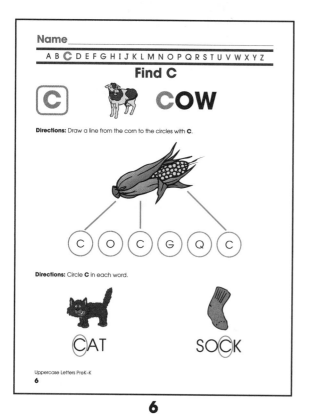

Answer Key

Name_____

A B C D **E** F G H I J K L M N O P Q R S T U V W X Y Z

Find E

E 🥚 **EGG**

Directions: Color the shapes with **E**.

Directions: Circle **E** in each word.

10
T(E)N

BELL

Uppercase Letters PreK–K
8

8

Name_____

A B C D E **F** G H I J K L M N O P Q R S T U V W X Y Z

Find F

F 🌀 **FAN**

Directions: Draw a line from the feather to the circles with **F**.

(E) (F) (F) (H) (F) (E)

Directions: Circle **F** in each word.

5
(F)IVE

LEA(F)

Uppercase Letters PreK–K
9

9

Name_____

A B C D E F **G** H I J K L M N O P Q R S T U V W X Y Z

Find G

G 👧 **GIRL**

Directions: Help the girl win the game. Color the boxes with **G**.

G	O	D	Q	D	C	D	O
G	C	C	Q	O	F	Q	A
G	A	Q	O	D	O	C	Q
G	C	O	Q	Q	C	D	O
G	G	G	G	G	G	G	G

Directions: Circle **G** in each word.

(G)UITAR

RU(G)

Uppercase Letters PreK–K
10

10

Name_____

A B C D E F G **H** I J K L M N O P Q R S T U V W X Y Z

Find H

H 🐴 **HORSE**

Directions: Color the shapes with **H**.

Directions: Circle **H** in each word.

(H)OUSE

(H)ORN

Uppercase Letters PreK–K
11

11

Answer Key

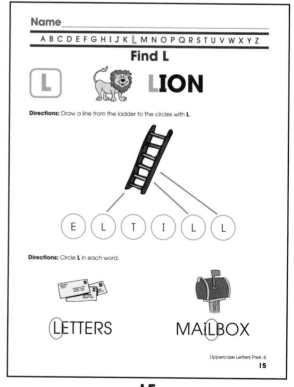

Answer Key

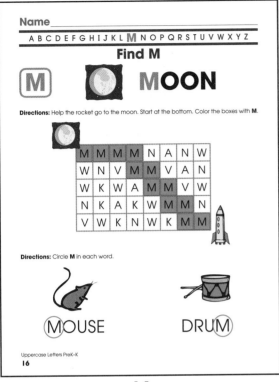

16

17

18

19

Answer Key

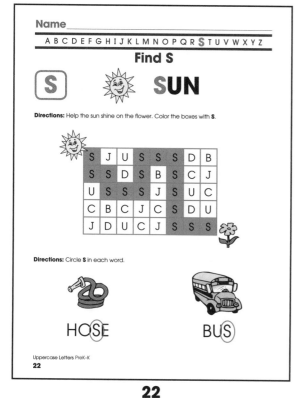

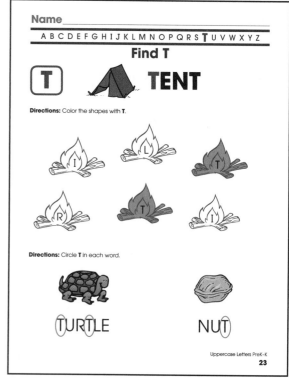

Answer Key

Name

A B C D E F G H I J K L M N O P Q R S T **U** V W X Y Z

Find U

U 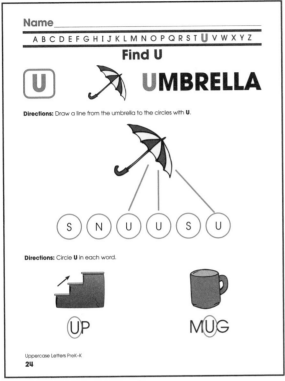 **U**MBRELLA

Directions: Draw a line from the umbrella to the circles with **U**.

(S) (N) (U) (U) (S) (U)

Directions: Circle **U** in each word.

(U)P   M(U)G

24

Name

A B C D E F G H I J K L M N O P Q R S T U **V** W X Y Z

Find V

V **V**AN

Directions: Help the van get home. Color the boxes with **V**.

V	W	N	M	V	V	V	V
V	N	W	X	V	W	N	V
V	W	X	N	V	N	N	V
V	V	V	V	V	W	X	V
M	W	N	X	W	M	N	V

Directions: Circle **V** in each word.

(V)ASE   (V)EST

25

Name

A B C D E F G H I J K L M N O P Q R S T U V **W** X Y Z

Find W

W **W**EB

Directions: Color the shapes with **W**.

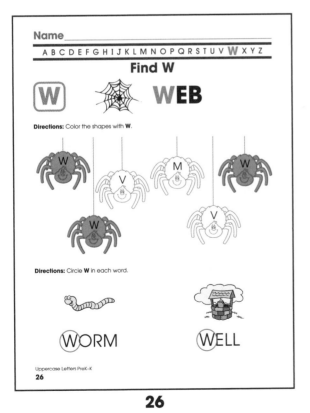

Directions: Circle **W** in each word.

(W)ORM   (W)ELL

26

Name

A B C D E F G H I J K L M N O P Q R S T U V W **X** Y Z

Find X

X FO**X**

Directions: Draw a line from the fox to the circles with **X**.

(X) (X) (S) (V) (N) (X)

Directions: Circle **X** in each word.

SI(X)   A(X)

27

Answer Key

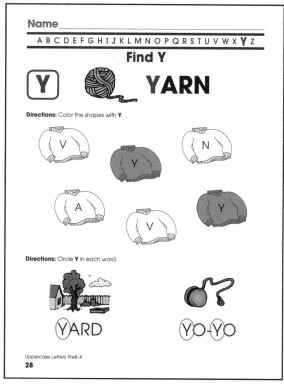

Name_____

A B C D E F G H I J K L M N O P Q R S T U V W X **Y** Z

Find Y

Y 🧶 **YARN**

Directions: Color the shapes with **Y**.

Directions: Circle **Y** in each word.

(Y)ARD   (Y)O-(Y)O

Uppercase Letters PreK-K
28

28

Name_____

A B C D E F G H I J K L M N O P Q R S T U V W X Y **Z**

Find Z

Z 🦓 **ZEBRA**

Directions: Help the zebra get to the zoo. Color the boxes with **Z**.

Z	Z	Z	Z	Z	Z	Z	X
X	A	V	N	X	N	Z	V
Z	Z	Z	Z	Z	Z	Z	V
Z	X	V	X	A	N	A	X
Z	Z	Z	Z	Z	Z	Z	Z

Directions: Circle **Z** in each word.

(Z)IPPER   PU(ZZ)LE

Uppercase Letters PreK-K
29

29

Name_____

A B C D E F G H I J K L M N O P Q R S T U V W X Y Z

Review

Directions: In each row, circle the letter that is the same as the first letter in the row.

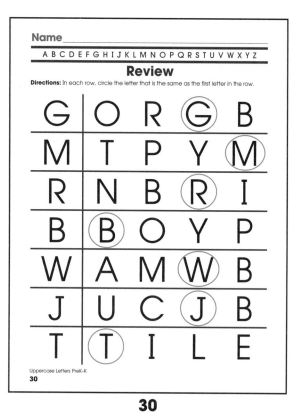

G	O	R	(G)	B
M	T	P	Y	(M)
R	N	B	(R)	I
B	(B)	O	Y	P
W	A	M	(W)	B
J	U	C	(J)	B
T	(T)	I	L	E

Uppercase Letters PreK-K
30

30

Name_____

A B C D E F G H I J K L M N O P Q R S T U V W X Y Z

Review

Directions: In each row, circle the letter that is the same as the first letter in the row.

A	Y	(A)	V	N
D	P	B	(D)	R
K	W	A	Z	(K)
F	E	T	H	(F)
Q	(Q)	O	G	C
C	O	G	(C)	Q
S	U	(S)	J	M

Uppercase Letters PreK-K
31

31

Answer Key

Name_____

A B C D E F G H I J K L M N O P Q R S T U V W X Y Z

I Know My ABCs

Directions: Help the dog find its house. Connect the letters in ABC order.

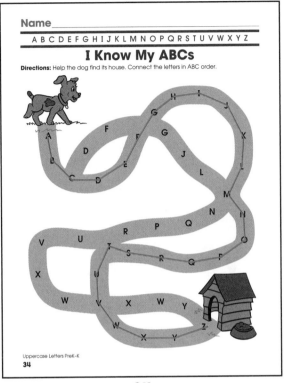

34

Name_____

A B C D E F G H I J K L M N O P Q R S T U V W X Y Z

I Know My ABCs

Directions: Connect the dots in ABC order.

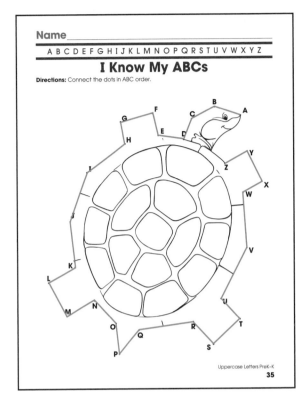

35

Name_____

A B C D E F G H I J K L M N O P Q R S T U V W X Y Z

Write Lines From Top to Bottom

Directions: Trace each line from top to bottom. Begin at ●.

36

Name_____

A B C D E F G H I J K L M N O P Q R S T U V W X Y Z

Write Lines From Left to Right

Directions: Trace each line from left to right. Begin at ●.

37

Answer Key

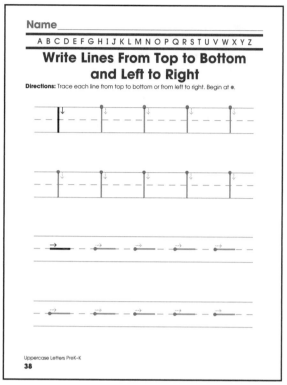

38

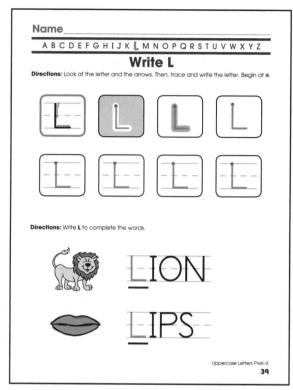

39

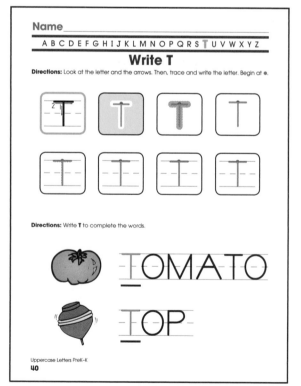

40

41

Answer Key

42

43

44

45

Uppercase Letters PreK–K

87

Answer Key

Write Slanted Lines

Directions: Trace each line from top to bottom. Begin at ●.

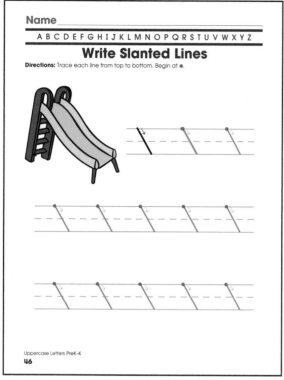

Uppercase Letters PreK–K
46

46

Write Slanted Lines

Directions: Trace each line. Begin at ●.

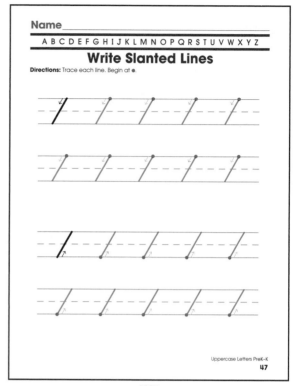

Uppercase Letters PreK–K
47

47

Write A

Directions: Look at the letter and the arrows. Then, trace and write the letter. Begin at ●.

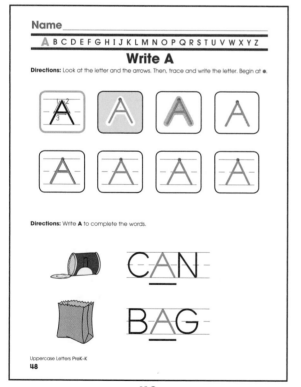

Directions: Write **A** to complete the words.

CAN

BAG

Uppercase Letters PreK–K
48

48

Write K

Directions: Look at the letter and the arrows. Then, trace and write the letter. Begin at ●.

Directions: Write **K** to complete the words.

DUCK

KING

Uppercase Letters PreK–K
49

49

Answer Key

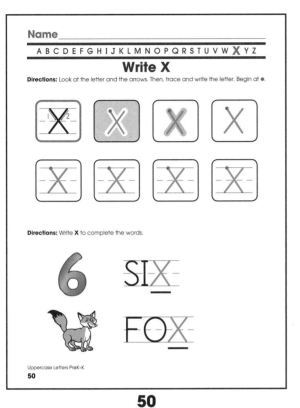

50

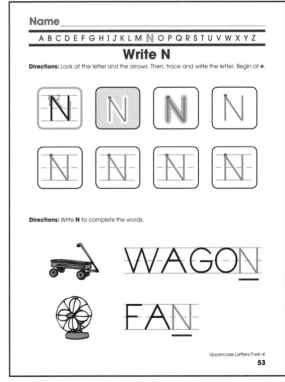

51

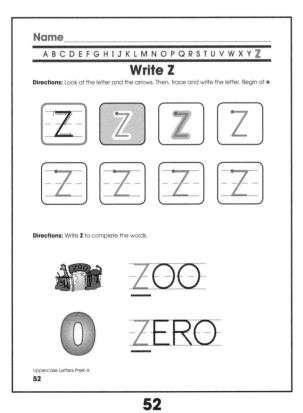

52

53

Answer Key

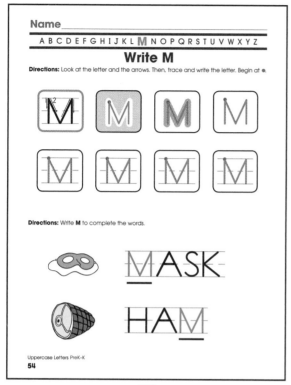

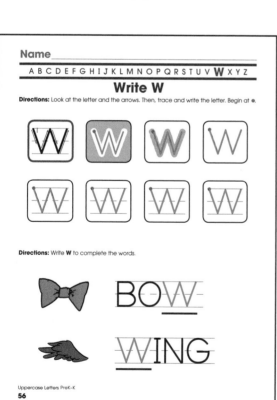

Answer Key

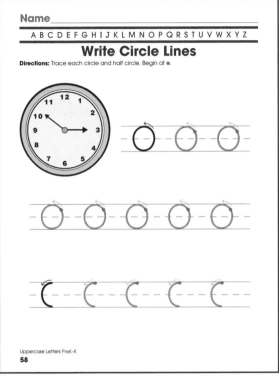

58

59

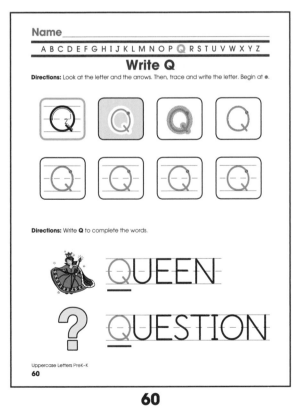

60

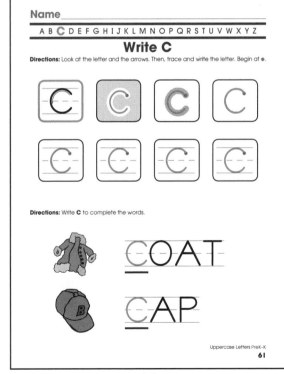

61

Answer Key

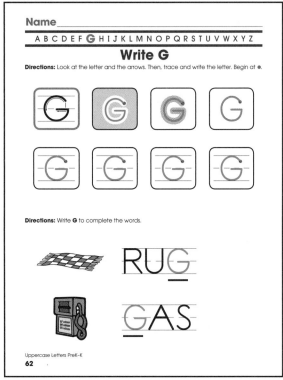

62

63

64

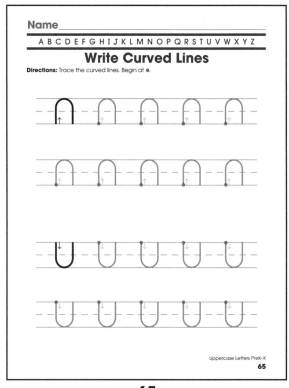

65

Answer Key

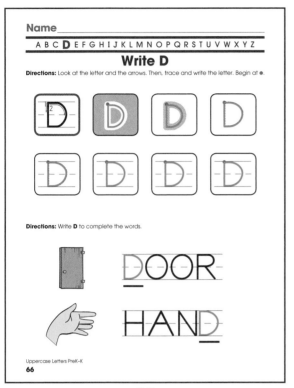

66

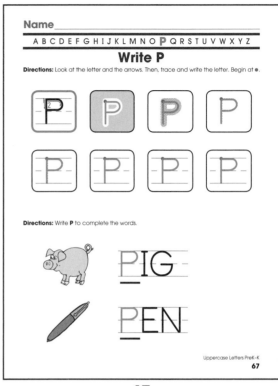

67

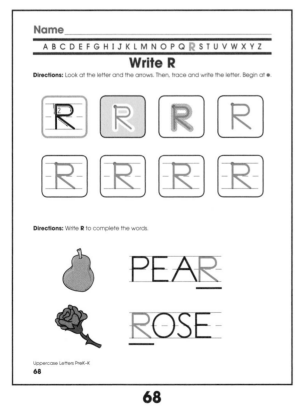

68

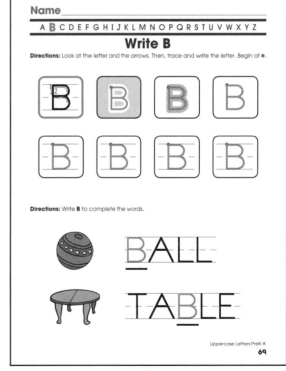

69

Answer Key

Uppercase Letters PreK–K
70

Name_____

A B C D E F G H I **J** K L M N O P Q R S T U V W X Y Z

Write J

Directions: Look at the letter and the arrows. Then, trace and write the letter. Begin at ●.

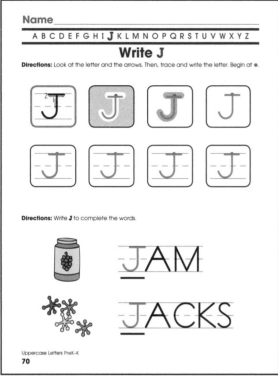

Directions: Write **J** to complete the words.

JAM

JACKS

70

Name_____

A B C D E F G H I J K L M N O P Q R S T **U** V W X Y Z

Write U

Directions: Look at the letter and the arrows. Then, trace and write the letter. Begin at ●.

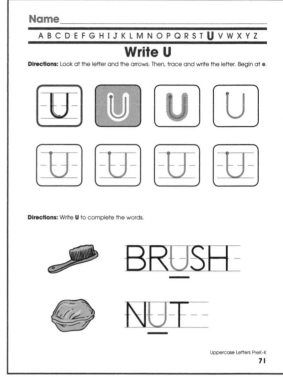

Directions: Write **U** to complete the words.

BRUSH

NUT

7l

Name_____

A B C D E F G H I J K L M N O P Q R **S** T U V W X Y Z

Write S

Directions: Look at the letter and the arrows. Then, trace and write the letter. Begin at ●.

Directions: Write **S** to complete the words.

SEAL

SEVEN

72

Name_____

A B C D E F G H I J K L M N O P Q R S T U V W X Y Z

Review

Directions: Write letters from the box to complete the words.

B   D   J   P   R   S   U

JEEP   DESK

BUS   ROOF

SOAP   PLUG

73

Answer Key

Name

A B C D E F G H I J K L M N O P Q R S T U V W X Y Z

Writing Review

Directions: Say the name of each picture. Write the uppercase letter that names its beginning sound.

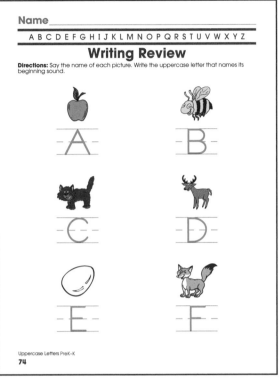

Name_____

A B C D E F G H I J K L M N O P Q R S T U V W X Y Z

Writing Review

Directions: Say the name of each picture. Write the uppercase letter that names its beginning sound.

A   B

C   D

E   F

Uppercase Letters PreK–K
74

74

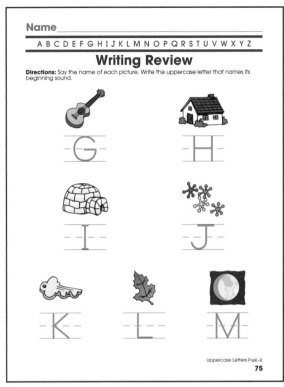

Name_____

A B C D E F G H I J K L M N O P Q R S T U V W X Y Z

Writing Review

Directions: Say the name of each picture. Write the uppercase letter that names its beginning sound.

G   H

I   J

K   L   M

Uppercase Letters PreK–K
75

75

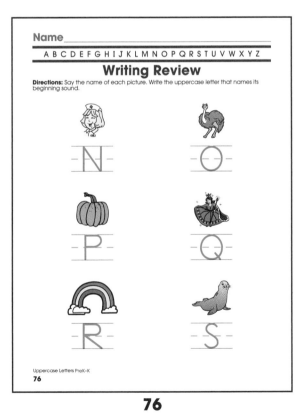

Name_____

A B C D E F G H I J K L M N O P Q R S T U V W X Y Z

Writing Review

Directions: Say the name of each picture. Write the uppercase letter that names its beginning sound.

N   O

P   Q

R   S

Uppercase Letters PreK–K
76

76

Name_____

A B C D E F G H I J K L M N O P Q R S T U V W X Y Z

Writing Review

Directions: Say the name of each picture. Write the uppercase letter that names its beginning sound.

T   U

V   W

X   Y   Z

Uppercase Letters PreK–K
77

77

Notes